The Visitor's Guide to
POINT REYES
NATIONAL SEASHORE

The Visitor's Guide to

POINT REYES
NATIONAL SEASHORE

by Alice F. Dalbey

THE CHATHAM PRESS, INC. RIVERSIDE CONNECTICUT

Cover photo: Drake's Beach and Cliffs by Homer Dalbey. All other
photographs by Alice F. Dalbey, Homer Dalbey, John V. Hinshaw and
courtesy of the National Park Service. Maps by Mary Lee Herbster.

Library of Congress Catalog Card Number: 73-89770
SBN: 85699-098-1

Printed in the United States of America.

CONTENTS

Monument commemorating the landing of Sir Francis Drake.

1. A WORLD APART

Point Reyes is a lonely land, a remote world where the drama of rugged headlands and surf-battered beaches is tempered by quiet estuaries, flowery meadows and peaceful forests.

People come here for all sorts of reasons: hikers to pace easy trails, beachcombers to prowl for driftwood and floats, fishermen to cast for ocean perch or sea trout. Birders scan the skies for tiny bluebirds or majestic golden eagles. Flower-lovers comb the headlands for scarce cobweb thistles and in spring enjoy meadows that glow with poppies and lupine. Photographers and painters compete to capture glistening cliffs and misty fogs.

But many visitors do absolutely nothing. For Point Reyes is an extraordinary place. Though within an hour's drive of San Francisco, the Point is removed from modern population pressures, a hundred-square-mile chunk of coastal California that is amazingly untouched and unsullied by civilization.

If you enjoy crowds, bright lights and night life, you won't find them here. But if you seek solitude and natural grandeur, Point Reyes will be your kind of country.

A Geological Island

Point Reyes is literally "a world apart," a huge hook-shaped peninsula separated from the continent by a great fracture in the earth's surface: the San Andreas Fault.

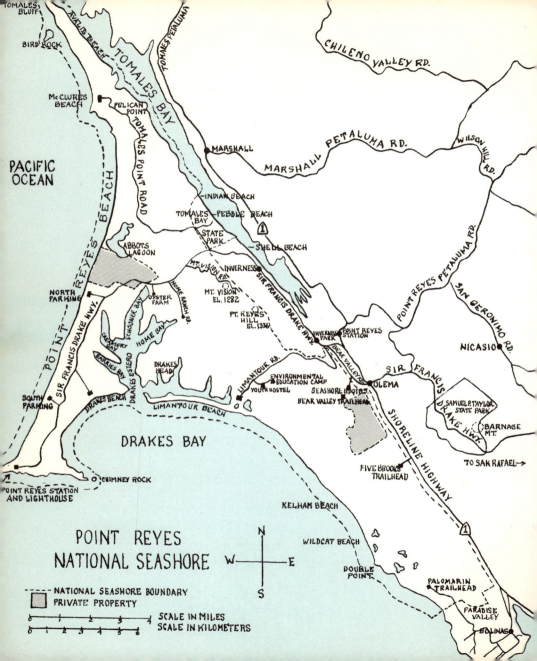

TOMALES BLUFF

BIRD ROCK

McCLURES BEACH

PELICAN POINT

PACIFIC OCEAN

ARCH BEACH

TOMALES BAY

TOMALES PETALUMA

CHILENO VALLEY RD.

MARSHALL

MARSHALL PETALUMA RD.

WILSON HILL RD.

TOMALES POINT ROAD

INDIAN BEACH

TOMALES BAY STATE PARK

PEBBLE BEACH

1

SHELL BEACH

POINT REYES BEACH

ABBOTS LAGOON

MT. VISION RD.

INVERNESS

HOME RANCH RD.

OYSTER FARM

MT. VISION EL. 1282

PT. REYES HILL EL. 1336

SIR FRANCIS DRAKE HWY.

POINT REYES PETALUMA RD.

SAN GERONIMO RD.

NICASIO

NORTH PARKING

SCHOONER BAY

HOME BAY

CREAMERY BAY

DRAKES ESTERO

DRAKES HEAD

DRAKES BEACH

LIMANTOUR RD.

LIMANTOUR BEACH

ENVIRONMENTAL EDUCATION CAMP

YOUTH HOSTEL

SEASHORE HDQTS.

BEAR VALLEY TRAILHEAD

INVERNESS PARK

POINT REYES STATION

BEAR VALLEY RD.

OLEMA

SIR FRANCIS DRAKE HWY.

SAMUEL P. TAYLOR STATE PARK

BARNAGE MT.

TO SAN RAFAEL →

SOUTH PARKING

POINT REYES STATION AND LIGHTHOUSE

CHIMNEY ROCK

DRAKES BAY

SHORELINE HIGHWAY

FIVE BROOKS TRAILHEAD

KELHAM BEACH

WILDCAT BEACH

1

DOUBLE POINT

PALOMARIN TRAILHEAD

PARADISE VALLEY

BOLINAS

POINT REYES
NATIONAL SEASHORE

N

W   E

S

– – – NATIONAL SEASHORE BOUNDARY

PRIVATE PROPERTY

SCALE IN MILES
SCALE IN KILOMETERS

The Northern California section of this tremendous rift, invisible except to the trained glance of the geologist, slices north from Bolinas Lagoon, passes beneath the grassy slopes of Olema Valley and the calm waters of Tomales Bay, and rims the coast for 160 miles until it swings out into the Pacific near Cape Mendocino.

West of the rift is Point Reyes, a geological "island" that scientists estimate is creeping northwest at an average rate of about two inches each year. While scientists debate the amount and rate of this displacement, the granite and shale rocks of Point Reyes are completely different from the Franciscan formation — a mix of sandstone, chert and serpentine — found on the eastern side of the fault on "mainland" California. The first site at which inland rocks match those of the Point is roughly three hundred miles south. Hence, some geologists believe Point Reyes has been on the move for the past eighty to one hundred million years.

Today, most of the Point is included in Point Reyes National Seashore and, for visitors, this geological isolation results in special fascinations.

Most dramatic is the coastline. At few other places in the world will you see such diverse ocean frontage. Rugged cliffs constantly are being eroded by the onslaught of the surf. Giant stacks — tall rock formations once part of the shore — stand out to sea, offering resting and sunning spots for birds and sea life. Beaches, from the eleven-mile-long, unbroken strand of Point Reyes Beach to secluded pocket coves accessible only at low tide, dot nearly ninety miles of coast. Vast spreading estuaries and salt marshes give shelter and food for schools of fish and flocks of birds.

Inland, often within a few hundred yards of the shore, are fresh-water lakes formed by natural dams — the results of the earth's folding and slipping. Here, too, are wide, windswept headlands and grassy meadows that are cloaked, almost year-round, in wildflowers.

Along Inverness Ridge, which forms the peninsula's spine, coastal hills soar more than a thousand feet into the misty sky, while dense forests of Douglas fir — akin to the woods of the Pacific Northwest and quite unlike other Central California woodlands — spike the ridge tops.

Thanks to the geological accident of the San Andreas Fault, the geography of Point Reyes has evolved during millions of years of shifting and folding of the earth's surface into a natural wonderland.

Across the Centuries

Thanks to historical accident, time has dealt gently with the Point. Stand today on the headlands overlooking Drake's Bay and, except for a few dairy ranches in the distance, you'll have much the same vista of ocean and cliffs, surf and sky, as did California's Coast Miwok Indians — once the sole proprietors of Point Reyes' splendid isolation.

After a millenium of peace, the Miwoks were disturbed by that magnificent British pirate-buccaneer, Sir Francis Drake. In 1579, after a successful expedition, Drake sought and found somewhere near Point Reyes a safe harbor in which to careen and repair his vessel, the *Golden Hinde*. Precisely where Drake landed, built a stone fort and erected a post bearing a brass plate claiming the country for Queen Elizabeth, is a hotly debated question. But the weight of

10

Drake's brass plate now on display at the University of California's Bancroft Library, Berkeley. Courtesy Bancroft Library. The text of the plate reads:

BEE IT KNOWNE VNTO ALL MEN BY THESE PRESENTS
IVNE.17.1579.
BY THE GRACE OF GOD AND IN THE NAME OF HERR
MAIESTY QVEEN ELIZABETH OF ENGLAND AND HERR
SVCCESSORS FOREVER I TAKE POSSESSION OF THIS
KINGDOME WHOSE KING AND PEOPLE FREELY RESIGNE
THEIR RIGHT AND TITLE IN THE WHOLE LAND VNTO HERR
MAIESTIES KEEPEING NOW NAMED BY ME AN TO BEE
KNOWNE VNTO ALL MEN AS NOVA ALBION.
G FRANCIS DRAKE

historical and nautical opinion favors Drake's Bay. This protected cove in the lee of Point Reyes Promontory is backed by tall white cliffs — probably those which caused Drake's homesick men to christen the land "Nova Albion" in remembrance of the cliffs of southeastern England.

Near the Information Center at Drake's Beach is a stone Maltese cross erected in memory of Drake's landing. A two-mile hike down the beach to the mouth of quiet Drake's Estero will bring you to the solid post and anchor set up by the Drake's Navigator's Guild at the point where the English sailor may have dropped anchor. But to see Drake's brass plate — and much scientific evidence supports its authenticity — you must travel to the Bancroft Library on the campus of the University of California at Berkeley. The plate was discovered in 1936, not at Drake's Bay as might be expected, but on San Quentin Point inside San Francisco Bay. If Drake left the plate at Drake's Bay, how did it get to San Quentin? Various explanations, some of them convincing, are given. But no one knows for sure. Perhaps the best evidence would be for the sands of Drake's Estero to shift suddenly during a winter storm and reveal a stone wall — the fort that Drake's men built .

Nearly a generation after Drake, the Miwoks played host again — this time to Sebastian Rodríguez Cermeño, a Portuguese captain in the hire of Spain, whose cargo-laden galleon *San Augustín* was blown ashore and demolished by heavy surf near the mouth of Drake's Estero in November, 1595. Iron spikes and Ming china, thought to be from the *San Augustín*, still occasionally appear in archaeological digs near Drake's Bay.

In 1603 the rugged promontory that hooks its way out into the Pacific finally was named and charted for navigators. A Spaniard, Sebastian Vizcaíno, sailed north from Mexico and rounded the great point on January 6, the Day of the Three Kings of the Nativity, and dubbed it *Punta de los Reyes*, the Point of Kings. Today purists, scholars and historians adhere to the correct Spanish pronunciation and say "Réy-es," but most people refer to the regal point as "Raise."

A commercial fishing boat at anchor beneath the same cliffs that sheltered Drake's *Golden Hinde*.

After Vizcaíno, Point Reyes sank into historical mists for nearly two centuries. In 1776, Spain established both a mission and a presidio on the bare headlands above San Francisco Bay. As the century turned, traders and sailors from most of the world's sea-faring nations arrived on California's northern coast to explore, and sometimes exploit, this new land. The widely scattered rancheros of Mexico and California, their experience and ambition broadened by this contact with other nations, fretted under the Spanish yoke. In 1821 they revolted, took possession of Mexico City and set up an independent Mexican empire.

The peaceful Miwoks of Point Reyes, little changed since the days of Drake, knew nothing of this. Through the early nineteenth century they watched whalers drop anchor in Drake's Bay and marveled at the swarthy Aleuts, in the pay of Russia, who swarmed beneath sheer cliffs off Point Reyes Promontory in quest of sea otter.

But in 1817 Spain and civilization overwhelmed the Miwoks. The Franciscan padres founded Mission San Rafael barely twenty-five miles inland from Point Reyes, and the Miwoks were encouraged to desert their lonely land for religious and agricultural domesticity. For a generation, Point Reyes was virtually uninhabited. When the mission era climaxed in 1834, the religious landholdings were "secularized" and appropriated by Mexico. A few Miwoks did straggle back to the Point — only to fall victim to disease and servitude and to disappear as a tribe.

During the Mexican years, a few vaguely defined Point Reyes land grants were made to rancheros and a few purchases, some by Americans, were authorized by the

One of the few dairy ranches remaining on the Point.

Mexican government. After the annexation of California by the United States in 1846, most of these early titles disappeared in a welter of legalities and bankruptcies. By 1860 most of Point Reyes was owned by the Shafter brothers, ex-Vermonters and prominent San Francisco attorneys, who leased ranches to tenants.

The Shafter family's grasp on Point Reyes was firm until the end of World War I when ranches began to be sold off, many of them to long-time tenants. Ranching, with an emphasis on dairy farming, continued to be the Point's major occupation, and the distant headlands were sprinkled with Holstein dairy cattle and white-faced Herefords. Point Reyes National Seashore was authorized in 1962 and though most of the Point is now within the Seashore, certain ranchers still retain rights to continue operations for a number of years.

Modern civilization has made remarkably little impact on the Point. The scattered adobes of early rancheros have disappeared. A few of the white, boxy ranch houses and huge barns built for Shafter tenants remain, but others and the fences that surround them are being removed by the National Park Service, as are traces of the hunting clubs that once flourished in Bear Valley and near Wildcat Beach.

Certain Douglas fir forests on the eastern slope of Inverness Ridge were logged in the 1950's. But the mild, year-round growing season encourages new forests and the worst lumbering scars are fast being covered.

The deer are thriving; the herds of harbor seals and sea lions are healthy and their rookeries protected from hunters. The thousands of ducks and migrating waterfowl that swarm the esteros from fall through spring are undisturbed. Even a few sea otters — descendents of the once huge colonies that were completely wiped out by Russian hunters — have been spotted swimming off the coast.

The Coast Miwoks and Drake's men might almost feel at home on Point Reyes today.

Reaching the Point

Point Reyes' first visitors came by sea and anchored in sheltered Drake's Bay, or searched north along the sands of Point Reyes Beach for the narrow, rock-bound passage around Tomales Point into the sunshine and quiet of Tomales Bay. Visitors still arrive by sea; some dock their cabin cruisers and sailboats at the Boatel in Inverness, others rock at anchor in the gentle swells off Drake's Beach.

But most contemporary visitors drive north from San

Francisco across the soaring Golden Gate Bridge on Highway 101 to the turnoff for Sir Francis Drake Boulevard and San Anselmo. This busy road threads through prosperous Marin County communities, crosses a low pass into San Geronimo Valley and then winds beneath the tall coast redwoods of Samuel P. Taylor State Park. A few miles beyond, as you top a sizeable hill, Point Reyes spreads out before you, a huge green land mass with slender firs piercing the sky and Tomales Bay glittering to the north.

If you have time to wander, follow California 1 north from the Golden Gate, visit the giant redwoods of Muir Woods National Monument, then twist along the cliffs and precipices that plunge down from Mt. Tamalpais — at 2571 feet, the highest peak in California's Coast Range — to the Pacific.

Visitors coming from the north often meander along California 1 and gain their first glimpses of the Point from Bodega Bay. Other winding roads lead west to Point Reyes from the inland communities of Novato and San Rafael.

Regardless of your route, find your way to Olema, a crossroads village on California 1, then go west on Bear Valley Road for a mile to Point Reyes National Seashore Headquarters — the informal gateway to the Point and the logical place to begin your visit.

Reaching Point Reyes requires a mental as well as a physical adjustment. From the crowded Bay Area cities you travel, in an hour or so, back through time. Here, waiting to be explored, is a land that looks much as it did when Sir Francis Drake arrived, and his chaplain Francis Fletcher described its inland reaches as, "a goodly country, and

A clear, summer's day on McClure's Beach.

fruitful soyle, stored with many blessings for the use of man."

Point Reyes Weather

Not all Fletcher's comments were favorable, however. He complained that during July Drake's men were plagued by "nipping cold . . . thicke mists and most stynkinge fogs."

Fog, especially from June through August, probably is the dominant weather feature of coastal Point Reyes. But the weather is notoriously unpredictable — it varies through the year, and often on the same day, from mild to wild.

In summer Point Reyes Beach, Tomales Point and the lighthouse promontory frequently are wrapped in heavy fog which may retreat briefly by mid-morning, only to come sweeping back across the headlands before dusk. The fog occurs because the ocean immediately along the coast is colder than it is farther out to sea. Moist, warm air from the western ocean, blown east by prevailing winds, cools over the chilly coastal waters which average 50 to 55 degrees. The result is a fog blanket that may extend fifty miles into the Pacific.

Nevertheless, Limantour and Drake's beaches may be sunny and pleasant, especially at midday when the fog recedes. Often when coastal fog is thickest, areas east of Inverness Ridge bask in warm sunshine and swimmers splash off sheltered beaches on Tomales Bay's western shore.

Autumn brings clear crisp days and refreshing showers to dusty paths; reawakens the pungent fragrances of pine and bay trees; touches the alders with gold; and flames in crimson one of Point Reyes' most enticing natural hazards — the bushes and twining vines of poison oak.

Point Reyes winter, the season of rains and ocean storms, extends from December through March. While stiff breezes blow year-round, usually from the northwest, in winter the wind vanes at the lighthouse sometimes veer into the south and a hundred-mile-an-hour gale hurls across the promontory, flinging water and sand in its wake.

The heaviest rains fall atop and to the east of Inverness Ridge; Bear Valley Headquarters averages 32 inches annually. Surprisingly, rainfall on the windy, fog-bound promontory is only about a third of that. A few inches of snow occasionally skiff the forests of the ridges, and on a few days each year frost may wither geraniums in Inverness gardens.

Winter also sets the stage for a spectacular show of bird and sea life. Migrating flocks clog the esteros and one annual Christmas bird count cited more than three hundred species — one of the highest counts in North America. Between December and February, California gray whales sound and spout in the surf off Point Reyes Beach as they pass on their migratory journey from the Bering Sea to Baja California.

Spring's primary gift is an unbelievably vivid wildflower display on meadows and headlands. Vast acres are sheeted with the gold of poppies and the pale lemon, blue and lavender of bush lupine. While this extravagant show peaks in late spring and early summer, Point Reyes has wildflowers year-round. Even in September, when Bear Valley trails are dusty and dry, lupines, buttercups, asters and poppies sparkle on gray-green, fog-dampened headlands.

Clothing for all Seasons

What to wear for Point Reyes weather? In winter, bring slickers and rain gear. In summer, the only safe course is to be prepared for everything, though heavy rains rarely fall at this time of year. Bring a windbreaker, sweaters to doff or don as you move with the sun and fog, and a scarf or cap as protection against the penetrating sea breeze. Canvas sneakers are favored footgear for beachcombing, and hiking boots with non-skid soles are recommended for inland trails and coastal rocks. Bring your bathing suit: there's always a chance of clear, still, warm weather, or you may locate a wind-free corner of beach.

"What's that thing?" Interpretive programs answer many questions from children and adults alike.

Ignore inland California weather. It may be 95 degrees and sunny in San Rafael but 50, foggy and blowing on Point Reyes Beach. Pessimists often phone before heading west. The rangers at Bear Valley Information Center will describe the Point's inland weather and those at Drake's Beach will give the coastal situation. But don't be surprised when you arrive an hour later to find that everything has changed completely.

The Amenities
Point Reyes and nearby villages are rural in atmosphere and resort accommodations are scarce. The only overnight facilities within the Park are primitive campgrounds reached by hiking trails. For information about services outside the Seashore, see Chapter 5 of this book.

Within the Seashore, the only restaurant is the Seashore Snack Bar at Drake's Bay, open from 11 A.M. to 5 P.M. daily (except Thanksgiving, Christmas and Near Year's Day), weather permitting. If you plan an all-day outing, be sure to bring a picnic. Also, stream water is not potable, so remember to fill your canteen. A camera (with plenty of film) and a pair of binoculars are valuable additions to any visit.

No fees are charged for admission, for participation in naturalist programs or for use of campgrounds within the Seashore.

Discovering Point Reyes

Point Reyes can become a lifetime adventure, a year-round spare-time devotion to walking trails, exploring beaches and getting to know the seasons and their special pleasures. You will discover when and where to see fawns, great blue herons, seal pups and migrating whales. You'll choose favorite spots — the broad summit meadows near Mount Wittenberg or rock-crusted Sculptured Beach. You'll debate between hiking boots or horses for back country treks and you'll dispute the beauties of Sky versus Wildcat camps. You may even fall victim to that most tantalizing and frustrating of hobbies — attempting to forecast Point Reyes weather.

Or you may develop a speaking acquaintance with the Point during a single day's trip in your car, for much of the Seashore's most dramatic scenery is accessible by auto. But be warned: Point Reyes' solitude, the richness of its natural life, its forests and flowers, have a way of growing on people. What begins as a casual interest may end as a life-long passion.

Point Reyes National Seashore may be divided into several regions, each with a personality all its own. These are Bear Valley to Limantour; Mt. Vision, Point Reyes Promontory; beaches and headlands; Tomales Point; and Back Country Trails and Camps.

National Park Service interpretive programs for these areas differ, depending on the season. So stop at one of the two Information Centers — Bear Valley or Drake's Beach — to pick up a schedule of events and to seek suggestions for what to do and see during your visit.

The "gateway" to Point Reyes National Seashore.

Hikers departing from Bear Valley Trailhead.

2. BEAR VALLEY TO LIMANTOUR

BEAR VALLEY

Bear Valley, a four-mile-long swath of forests and meadows that bisects Inverness Ridge between Olema Valley and the coast, is one of the most popular regions of the Seashore. Clustered near the valley's eastern entrance, a mile west of Olema, are old ranch residences and barns, relics of the days when Bear Valley Ranch was a prosperous dairy farm.

Today these ranch buildings are Headquarters offices for the National Seashore, and Bear Valley Ranch, so-named for the California black bears that prowled here as late as the 1890's, is the main "gateway" to the Seashore. The Park has no formal entrance gate.

Bear Valley is the best place to begin your visit to Point Reyes and a tour of the area near the Information Center will introduce you to the Seashore and make your visit more enjoyable.

Bear Valley Information Center
The Bear Valley Information Center, a small white building set in the midst of old ranch structures, is the primary source for information about the Seashore. The Center is open daily from 8 A.M. until 5 P.M., later in summer. You can pick up schedules here for National Park Service interpretive programs throughout the Park. The Center also has a

selection of books, maps and pamphlets — a few are free — plus exhibits and photographs that explain the geology, geography, flora and fauna of the Seashore.

Across a little creek in a grassy clearing behind the Center is a small amphitheater, the site of ranger lectures. Other visitor conveniences — telephones, restrooms, water fountain and a parking lot — are close by.

But the most fascinating attraction on display in the Information Center is the seismograph, a sensitive instrument that registers the slightest quiver of the San Andreas Fault, as well as other jolts and movements of the earth. Charts showing recent quake activity are posted nearby.

Morgan Horse Farm

As you tour the Bear Valley Headquarters area, you are sure to hear, amid the bird calls and the wind sighing in the tall firs, the gentle nicker of horses. For Point Reyes has a unique attraction: the only Morgan horse breeding farm in the National Park Service.

Here, where Mexican rancheros ran herds of wild horses and turn-of-the-century American ranchers staged rodeos and trotting races, is a band of sleek mares and colts — Morgan horses, carefully bred and painstakingly trained.

The primary reason for the horse farm is to give city children an opportunity to pet a foal and to see the handsome animals trained. A secondary purpose is to breed and train Morgans for use as patrol animals in national parks throughout the U.S.

The best places to see, pet and photograph the Morgans are the lot behind the big red barn (once the Bear Valley

Morgan colts bred and raised for service in the national parks.

A horse training demonstration.

Ranch dairy barn) by the Information Center and in the spreading pasture opposite the picnic area.

Morgan horses, the first distinctively American breed, are noted for their stamina, calmness and intelligence. All Morgans are descended from Justin Morgan, a notable stallion that was born in Massachusetts but lived most of his thirty-two years — from 1789 to 1821 — in Vermont.

The Point Reyes farm is a combined effort. A stallion and mare were donated, and other mares loaned, to the Park by members of the Northern California Morgan Horse Club with the agreement that every second colt belonged to the Park Service. The first stud colt, born in 1970, was christened *Los Reyes Terremoto* —The King's Earthquake — and each Seashore colt born since then has been given a name beginning with "Los Reyes."

Horse training and riding demonstrations sometimes are planned during summer weekends, and special sessions are arranged for visiting groups. Phone Headquarters at least three days ahead of your visit to make arrangements.

Blacksmith Shop

In recognition of Point Reyes' agricultural and pastoral past, the National Park Service has built a working blacksmith shop — complete with anvil, forge and a collection of farrier's equipment. Located behind the Information Center, the shop is open most weekends. On weekdays, you can peer through the gate to see old tools. Parked near the shop are antique farm machines — a mower, hay rake and grain drill — similar to those used on early ranches here.

Demonstrations showing the machinery and blacksmith shop in action sometimes are scheduled for summer weekends. Special showings will be arranged for groups of twenty or more visitors. To make arrangements, phone Headquarters at least three days ahead of your visit.

Environmental Study Area Trail

Designed primarily as an outdoor classroom for teachers and school groups, the two-mile ESA Trail begins at the big red barn and circles forty acres of forest, meadow, marsh and stream course.

School classes, using a "Teacher's Guide" and "Student Workbook" written by Park Service naturalists and keyed to numbered posts along the trail, usually occupy a full day studying the area.

Individuals, families and small groups also hike this route. A thoughtful tour of the ESA Trail — taken in company with the "Guide" and "Workbook" which are sold at the Information Center — is not only the best possible introduction to the ecology and environment of inland Point Reyes, but also is an excellent refresher course in elementary botany and zoology.

Earthquake Trail

One of the most exciting walks in the Seashore is the Earthquake Trail — a half-mile path that traces the course of the San Andreas Fault as it cuts its way through the Bear Valley Headquarters area.

To engage in a bit of brinksmanship, find the trail sign several yards north of the trailhead, walk down the road-

The line of posts in the foreground marks the San Andreas fault along earthquake trail.

way toward the blacksmith shop, then swing south along Bear Valley Creek. Take time to read the explanatory signs on this self-guiding trail and ponder the exhibit panel that explains continental drift and shows where Point Reyes may be two hundred million years from now.

The Olema Valley rift zone — the low-lying area stretching north and south between Tomales Bay and Bolinas Lagoon — was the epicenter of the great San Francisco earthquake. On that April day in 1906, Point Reyes took a great leap northward — as much as fifteen to twenty feet. Evidences of that jolt are all about you at Bear Valley and the most significant ones are pointed out on the Earthquake Trail. The blue-painted fence posts mark the actual fault line. Watch for weathered old fence posts which were offset by the quake and for a diverted creek. These physical evidences are enhanced by exhibits of photographs taken shortly after the shake. The big red barn was dragged sixteen feet off its foundations.

A stroll along this trail will help you comprehend the whys, wherefores and results of earthquakes. Unfortunately, say the Park Service naturalists, no one can yet predict the *when* of a quake, but "one *will* happen," since the San Andreas Fault is a very much alive, exceedingly active fracture in the earth's crust.

Picnic Area

One of the most peaceful spots is the nearby picnic area where Douglas firs and California bay trees shade picnic tables. (No wood fires are permitted here.) Drive a quarter of a mile beyond the Information Center, park in the lot at the trailhead and carry your lunch basket in among the trees.

The picnic area is an ideal place for lazy bird-watching. Settle back on a blanket, binoculars at the ready, and you'll probably see fly catchers, sparrows of all descriptions, woodpeckers and at least one red-tailed hawk. Wait an hour or so, especially in spring, and a great blue heron, perhaps even a snowy egret, will sail through the tree tops above you.

Beyond the picnic area is a wide meadow, dotted with rounded live oaks and bays, which was cleared of brush years ago and used by Point Reyes ranching families as a race track and rodeo grounds. Today visitors fly kites and play catch on this broad, grassy plain.

Bear Valley Trailhead

The back country of Point Reyes Seashore has two major access points — Palomarin Trailhead, in the southern part of the Park, and Bear Valley Trailhead, a quarter of a mile beyond the Information Center. Bear Valley is the more popular of the two. (For a detailed description of the trails, see Chapter 4 of this book.)

For a short walk into the forest that blankets Inverness Ridge, and for a glimpse of the country you might visit on more remote trails, hike out the Bear Valley Trail to Divide Meadow. After a gentle mile-and-a-half climb along a wide, stream-side path that winds through ferns and flowers, you reach a broad, sloping vale ringed with firs. In spring, Divide Meadow is awash with wildflowers, and if you arrive in early morning or late afternoon you probably will see deer feeding on the nearby slopes.

Woodpecker Trail

To combine birding with an easy walk, locate the Woodpecker Trail sign near the Bear Valley Trailhead and saunter up the slope into the forest. Pick up a free leaflet with explanations keyed to the numbered signs along the path, and guide yourself on a half-mile, never-fail bird walk.

Acorn or California woodpeckers, gregarious birds that drill holes in tree trunks and then cram them full of acorns against the winter season, live here by the hundred. While the noisy woodpeckers are the feature attractions of this path, the trail is also planned as an introductory walk into the Point Reyes Woodlands.

LIMANTOUR

Limantour is an area — a beach, a sand spit, an estero. Leading to it is Limantour Road which departs from Bear Valley Road north of the Seashore Headquarters to curve eight miles up and over the ridge, then down to Drake's Bay.

This drive offers the best opportunity in the Seashore to see a cross section of Point Reyes forests and grasslands. You climb from broad inland meadows dotted with oaks and bays to the Douglas firs and Bishop pines of higher elevations, then descend into brushy headlands that roll toward the sea. Stop near the summit and look west for views of the coast and east for vistas of Olema Valley and the village of Point Reyes Station.

Trails

Bayview-Muddy Hollow Trail. A mile below the summit, park behind the rail fence that runs near an old quarry scar to reach this trail. The 3.5 mile walk, a haunt of birders and wildflower lovers, parallels a stream (wear waterproof boots in the wet season), threads downhill through pines and grassy meadows, with frequent panoramas of Drake's Estero, then edges past several ponds to end at Limantour parking area. To hike only the lower portion of this path, continue down Limantour Road to Home Ranch Road, turn north for .2 mile to the junction with Muddy Hollow Trail.

Point Reyes Hill Trail. This is a steep, 3.5 mile climb from the Muddy Hollow parking area through meadows and a

The Laguna Ranch Youth Hostel.

Bishop pine forest to the summit of Point Reyes Hill. At 1336 feet, it is the second highest point in the Seashore.

Glenbrook Trail. From the junction with Home Ranch Road, hike north about a mile and a half to Glenbrook. This path, a favorite with birders, then follows a ridgetop for about a mile to Limantour Estero. A detailed guide to these and other short estero trails is available for a small fee at Bear Valley Information Center.

Laguna Ranch American Youth Hostel

Swing south at the intersection of Limantour and Home Ranch roads, and you enter a protected valley where the refurbished residence and barn of the old Laguna Ranch provide overnight accommodations for hostelers. The hostel is open year-round, seven days a week, from 4:30 P.M. to

9:00 A.M.; reservations are necessary and stays are limited to three days.

Point Reyes Environmental Education Camp

A quarter of a mile up the valley from the hostel is a primitive camp, open on a reservations-only basis to teachers and classes who come to study aspects of the Seashore. Phone Headquarters for information. From the camp and the hostel, a trail leads past a bird-rich marsh to Limantour Beach, then connects with the southward-bound Coast Trail.

Limantour Beach and Estero

Limantour Road ends at a parking area three hundred yards from a wide, white beach backed by low grassy dunes that are pocked with sheltered spots to sun and picnic. Limantour Beach is one of two places in the Seashore where wading and swimming usually are safe — Drake's Beach is the other.

While many visitors come here to sun or stroll, others come to see Limantour's greatest attraction: the bird life of the estero. The west arm of Limantour Beach is a broad sandspit that protects an estero with ten miles of shoreline. Here, say the Park naturalists, is the best place in the Seashore to see birds, especially between November and March.
Limantour Estero is one of the few marshes on the Pacific Coast that has not been dammed or seriously altered by man; wintering and migrant shore and water birds come here by the thousands to rest and feed.

Dunes Nature Trail

To observe the birds, as well as to study the delicate plants and to grasp the complex ecology of the Limantour estero, take this mile-long self-guiding nature walk from the parking area. The estero is a quiet place — yet the surf rumbles beyond the dunes like distant thunder and the mud flats echo with shrill cries of gulls and sandpipers. You will see ducks, plovers and an occasional brown pelican come here to fish. At trail's end you may glimpse harbor seals resting on the sandspit.

Shuttle Bus

On summer weekends, usually between July 4 and Labor Day, a small bus travels between Bear Valley Trailhead and the Limantour parking area. By parking at either place, then riding the bus to intervening spots, you may make long trips — part hiking, part riding — through this region of the Seashore. For specific bus schedules and for suggestions about trails, inquire at the Bear Valley Information Center.

3. MOUNT VISION, POINT REYES PROMONTORY AND TOMALES POINT

MOUNT VISION

Point Reyes Seashore has three "mountains:" 1407-foot Mount Wittenberg, 1336-foot Point Reyes Hill and 1282-foot Mount Vision. The summits of Wittenberg and Point Reyes Hill are reached only by trail, but a well-surfaced, scenic road (no trailers or busses permitted) winds up Mt. Vision.

Follow Sir Francis Drake Highway through Inverness, then up and over the ridge until you reach, on the left, a small blue sign for "Mount Vision Overlook." Twist your way up through meadow and forest. Park at the top, by the locked gate, then take an easy top-of-the-world stroll around the hilltop. To the south and west are panoramas of esteros and ocean; to the north and east are spreading views of Tomales Bay, the Olema Valley, the community of Point Reyes Station and the rolling hills of "mainland" California.

In spring and early summer, the slopes of Mount Vision are decked with the deep purple blooms of ceanothus — a tall, fragrant bush that is ancestor to the dooryard lilac — and the meadows glisten with poppies, lupines and asters.

These meadows are a favorite feeding area for Point Reyes deer. Arrive in the early morning or late afternoon

The Johnson oyster farm.

and you may see the native black-tailed deer, plus two exotic species introduced to the Point in the 1940's. Axis deer, natives of India, have reddish-brown coats dotted with white spots. Fallow deer, natives of Mediterranean countries, usually are light colored — white or buff — and have large, flat palmate antlers like those of the moose.

DRAKE'S ESTERO

About a mile west of the Mount Vision turnoff from Sir Francis Drake Highway is a left turn that will take you to Drake's Estero Trail. From the parking area at the trailhead, a 4.6-mile path leads through marsh, meadow and a one-time Christmas tree farm along the shores of Home Bay (named in the early days for nearby Home Ranch) which is the eastern arm of Drake's Estero.

With nearly three times the shoreline of Limantour Estero, Drake's has the same fascination for birds and, in addition, has a spectacular show of sea life. The estero is a nursery for leopard sharks and on a bright clear day with

the sun shining into the water, you will see hundreds of these predators, plus winged stingrays, swimming in Home Bay. A herd of harbor seals resides near the mouth of the estero. Don't be surprised when a curious one pokes his head above the surf to peer at you.

Drake's Estero, unlike Limantour, has been used by man. A century ago, shallow-draft coastal schooners loaded with cattle and dairy products — Point Reyes butter brought premium prices — engaged in lively trade with San Francisco. Near the point between Home and Schooner bays notice the old pier pilings just under the water.

While the estero bays are no longer navigable because heavy grazing and increased erosion have silted once-passable channels, they still are serving man. The wickets you see are oyster racks — growing beds for the large Japanese oysters harvested and sold commercially at the Johnson Oyster Farm. (Oysters are sold to visitors daily from 8 A.M. to 4:30 P.M. at the Schooner Bay farm, which is reached from Sir Francis Drake Highway, a short distance past the Estero Trail turn.)

Point Reyes Beach viewed from the promontory.

POINT REYES BEACH

The long, western shore of Point Reyes, with its beaches, headlands and rocks that confront the brutal surf and storms of the Pacific, encompasses much of the Seashore's most magnificent scenery.

Beyond the quiet upper reaches of Drake's Estero, Sir Francis Drake Highway slowly climbs past dairy ranches and a forest of poles and wires that marks R.C.A. and A.T.&T. overseas communications stations to wide, sandy meadows and the turn for Point Reyes Beach North. A second access road leading to Point Reyes Beach South is three miles beyond.

This vast eleven-mile-long beach of coarse, gray, granitic sand sweeps south to the promontory and north to Kehoe Beach. Between these landmarks visitors beachcomb, surf-cast, picnic, seek sheltered sunning spots or comb the dunes for the beach daisies, maritime poppies and bush lupine that bloom much of the year.

Facilities at both North and South Point Reyes Beach include large parking lots and restrooms but no bath-houses. *Swimming and wading are extremely dangerous and many people have drowned here.* The heavy surf crashes against the beach, creating a steep drop-off and a strong undertow that defeats the strongest swimmers. To enjoy this roaring surf, sit at a safe distance and watch it hiss, boil, curl and change shades of blue and green — but stay beyond reach of the treacherous waves.

ABOVE: The Kenneth C. Patrick Information Center. BELOW: Drake's Beach from the overlook. RIGHT: surfers brave the autumn wind and waves.

DRAKE'S BEACH

At the sign for Drake's Beach, leave Sir Francis Drake Highway and swing down to the sheltered cove, beach and the Kenneth C. Patrick Information Center at Drake's Bay. The Center, open daily from 8 A.M. to 5 P.M. in summer (winter hours are variable), has restrooms, showers, a book shop, a lunch room and telephones. Ranger-naturalists on duty will answer questions and tell you about interpretive programs throughout the Seashore.

Looming above Drake's Beach are the white cliffs — the shining clay banks, visible for miles, that are the most convincing evidence that Sir Francis Drake did careen his *Golden Hinde* nearby. At no other place on the California coast, within the proper latitudes, are such cliffs found. For a sea gull's view of the cliffs, the bay and the beach below, climb the hill opposite the Information Center to Drake's Bay Overlook.

The white cliffs protect Drake's Beach from the stiff northwest winds and make it, and Limantour Beach, the only two places in the Seashore calm enough, and sometimes warm enough, for safe swimming. No lifeguards are on duty here, however. Visitors also fish and beachcomb along the broad sweep of Drake's Beach.

POINT REYES PROMONTORY

To visit the massive Point itself, continue south on Sir Francis Drake Highway four and a half miles beyond the Drake's Beach intersection. As you drive through a dairy ranch, ignore the main road and turn left on a narrow, one-lane track through a ranch gate, then continue .3 mile to the Otter View parking area. From these cliffs, you gaze down on rocks that stud the blunt, southern tip of the Point.

Chimney Rock

To reach Chimney Rock, stay with this narrow ranch road an additional .3 mile, park and meander along the cattle path that climbs the hill behind a ranger residence. An easy, mostly level walk through a flower-strewn pasture offers you views of Drake's Bay and the white cliffs six miles north across the water. Below you, commercial fishing boats often ride at anchor; during the salmon season, as many as fifty may take refuge in this quiet harbor. Beyond the fishing docks, which are closed to the public, is a one-time Coast Guard life-saving station. Notice the iron tracks from the Station into the Bay. These are for surf-boats, the heavy rescue craft manned by Coast Guard crews trained to save men from storm-tossed ships.

As you approach land's end, another overlook hedged by a rail fence offers not only views of the promontory but on clear days, a magnificent full-circle prospect of the ocean, Drake's Bay, Limantour and the southern coast of the Seashore. Chimney Rock, smeared white with guano,

Sea lions at Sea Lion Cove.

stands at the promontory's tip — a navigator's landmark for the entrance to Drake's Bay.

The rocky shoreline at the base of the cliffs along Point Reyes Promontory is a Research Natural Area, off-limits to visitors. *All these cliffs are exceedingly hazardous. Stay behind fences and do not attempt to climb up or down the crumbly banks.*

Sea Lion Cove

To observe one of the most remarkable sea-life habitats on the Pacific Coast, continue west toward the Point on Sir Francis Drake Highway. Stop at the next wide place in the road, follow the wooden steps to an overlook part way down the cliff and peer over to the rocky coves below. This is the year-round home for a herd of California and Stellar sea lions that, during spring and fall migrations, sometimes numbers in the hundreds. Bring binoculars and look carefully. You may spot a giant Stellar bull — they sometimes weigh a ton — sunning himself on the rocks.

RIGHT: The twin bulbs inside the lens of Point Reyes Light. Stand holds an oil lantern used during power failures. BELOW: Point Reyes Lighthouse overlooking the sea.

Point Reyes Lighthouse

The next and final stop on this high, ridge road is the parking area for the lighthouse, Point Reyes' most historic structure.

Point Reyes cliffs and reefs have always been hazardous for sailors. Records show that 57 ships — from the *San Augustín* in 1595 to the *San Domenico* in 1935 — have been wrecked nearby. In 1870 the Coast Guard perched a lighthouse on the farthest tip of the promontory, three hundred feet above the surf, then imported a three-ton lens with more than a thousand pieces of glass that, when powered by a gas flame, could be seen twenty-four miles out to sea. The great light bears a shining brass plate stamped "Lighthouse Board, Barbier and Fenestre, Paris 1867," and is decorated with an etched American Eagle. It was brought around the Horn in a sailing vessel, then dragged to the Point by ox cart. While this powerful light is still operative today, it has been replaced by an automatic beacon.

The trek to the lighthouse is not for the faint-hearted or weak-kneed. Four hundred shallow, concrete steps lead down the cliff. But rewards include close looks at curving lines of foam tossed by currents breaking around the Point, birds swooping over rocks and waves, and in spring and fall, views of migrating whales sounding in the surf. As you climb up or down the steps, notice the lichen on the cliffs, and the poppies, wild strawberries and tiny succulents that bloom here because of the continual dampness. The foghorn, which operates an average of sixty-two days each year, is deafening.

Since the hike down to the light is dangerous in fog and

wind, the lighthouse is open only when the National Park Service staff and the variable weather permit.

Take time to enjoy the view near the parking area but stay on established trails; people have been killed while attempting to climb down these cliffs. To the north is the unbroken sweep of Point Reyes Beach. On a clear day and with binoculars, you can see the Golden Gate Bridge and San Francisco to the southeast. And twenty-five miles out to sea due south of the Point are the Farallon Islands, today a refuge for birds and seals, but once, in distant geological history, part of the same land mass as Point Reyes.

TOMALES POINT

As you travel Sir Francis Drake Highway west from Inverness, take the first right-hand fork inside the Seashore boundary, swing north on Tomales Point Road through open Bishop pine forest, past the turn for Tomales Bay State Park, into one of Point Reyes' most remote and scenic regions.

Abbotts Lagoon

About three and a half miles along, look for a handsome green and white ranch house, and park a few hundred yards beyond it in the area reserved for visitors to Abbotts Lagoon. This large, brackish estero is separated from the northern reaches of Point Reyes Beach by a giant sandbar — sometimes breached in stormy weather — and serves as a haven for migrating waterfowl. Canoeists can make a short portage from the parking area to paddle on the lagoon.

Kehoe Beach

About two miles further north you will find the trailhead for Kehoe Beach. As you pass through the narrow opening that marks the trail's start, veer to your right and search the large sandstone outcropping for smooth oval depressions — Indian mortars, relics of the Coast Miwoks. This rock must have been a favorite kitchen area — acorns pounded in mortars like these were a staple of the Miwok diet.

Kehoe Beach, a two-mile walk from the road and a prime place to search for fishing floats or driftwood after winter storms, is at the northern end of Point Reyes Beach.

McClure's Beach

Tomales Point Road ends at the parking area for McClure's Beach. To visit this curving, rock-bound cove, hike a half mile downhill between dunes draped with flowers. The show is at its best in June when, within a few feet, you may discover lavender, yellow paintbrush, yellow lupine, the rare cobweb thistle and, if you search diligently, the spotted cups of godetia.

While crashing surf and hidden rocks make the sandy crescent of McClure's Beach unsafe for swimming or wading, it is a favorite region for tide-pool exploring. At low tide, walk south along the beach through the narrow passage of Elephant Rock. Here, exposed to the ocean's constant washing, are rocks and pools that are home for abalone, barnacles, star fish, mussels and sea urchins. Observe but do not disturb this sea life. Abalone pickers clad in wet suits sometimes search the rocks, and surf fishermen cast heavy lines from the beach.

Air view of Tomales Point.

Tomales Point Trail

The five-mile-long tip of the Seashore reaching north from McClure's Beach is reserved for hikers. While the trail to Tomales Point is long — ten plus miles round trip — it is mostly level and offers exciting ocean and bay views.

For nearly four miles you tread the road that once connected the Upper and Lower Pierce Point ranches, model dairy farms owned and operated for nearly a century by the Pierce family. The white-faced Herefords that graze these wide pastures today soon will be gone, and the range will return to its native brush. Future plans of the National Park Service include establishment of a tule elk herd here. The elk, like the grizzlies, were Point Reyes natives that were exterminated during the nineteenth century.

As the land narrows, you have vistas east across Tomales Bay of the villages, ranches and hills of "mainland" California and to the west of the Pacific. The road dwindles to a path near Bird Rock, a tall stack thick with cormorants.

Beyond Bird Rock, bear left past a wind-sculptured cypress, then pick your way through waist-high lupine and coyote bush toward the cliffs and headlands that overlook the narrow, often fog-bound inlet to Tomales Bay.

Spread your lunch on the protected northern slope and enjoy a magnificent show of bird and sea life. Brown pelicans soar below you in long, undulating rows; cormorants, snaky necks weaving, rise in flotillas off rocky ledges; gulls wheel in the sun; and you may see a harbor seal or a sea lion fishing in the wild surf below. If you are very lucky, you may spot a rare tufted puffin preening himself on a rocky ledge — your reward for having hiked to Tomales Point.

4. BACK COUNTRY TRAILS AND CAMPS

For many Point Reyes visitors, the ultimate adventure is a hike into the back country that extends from Limantour Road to the Seashore's southern border. Interlocking trails of varying length and difficulty span thousands of acres of forest, meadow, headland and beach that are closed to motorized vehicles and reserved exclusively for hikers, backpackers and horsemen.

Trailheads

These backcountry trails are entered by way of three main trailheads. Bear Valley Trailhead just beyond the Information Center is the most popular, especially for day hikers. Five Brooks Trailhead, located off California 1 three miles south of Olema, offers riding stables and access to the central portion of the back country area. Palomarin Trailhead, the southern entrance to back country trails, is reached by taking the road to Bolinas off California 1. Just before the town, turn right on Mesa Road and follow it to the end where there are parking spaces but no facilities. All hikers planning to be out more than one day are required to register at Bear Valley Information Center, and camping is permitted only in designated camp sites.

Be sure to don comfortable shoes, to carry a jacket and to fill your water bottle since stream water in the Seashore is not potable. Check your map for distances and consult a ranger-naturalist about alternate or circle trips; he may suggest especially scenic or interesting routes.

While hiking, stay on marked, well-defined trails; old roads and cattle paths that appear passable may not be maintained. Be wary of cliffs; soil and rocks that seem firm may be crumbly! If you plan to prowl tide pools or pocket beaches, check tidal timetables in local newspapers or with rangers at Bear Valley; be aware of the tide, so you won't be trapped on a reef or rock.

NORTHERN TRAILS: BEAR VALLEY TO LIMANTOUR

Bear Valley Trail

For an easy introduction to the joys of Point Reyes hiking, begin with Bear Valley Trail, the most popular all-day hike in the Seashore. Bear Valley and Coast trails, though rough in spots, are the only Seashore trails suitable for bicycling. If you bring or rent a bicycle, however, be sure it is sturdy and in good condition. The trails are rough, giving a bumpy ride and an occasional flat tire or other damage.

The broad Bear Valley Trail joins a creek near the trailhead, winds through woods of oak, bay and buckeye, and climbs gently into the Douglas fir forest with its dense undergrowth of ferns and wildflowers. Divide Meadow, a good goal for a short hike, is 1.6 miles from the trailhead. The trail continues south from there through the forest to an intersection with Glen Trail and Coast Creek, then veers west through brushy headlands to Arch Rock Overlook, high above the surf, 4.4 miles from the Bear Valley Trailhead.

Arch Rock at the end of Bear Valley Trail.

Arch Rock. The view from Arch Rock Overlook, at the end of Bear Valley Trail, is spectacular and it is a perfect place for a picnic. To the west rises the bulky Point Reyes Promontory; to the north are the rocky coastline and the white cliffs of Drake's Beach. South are offshore rocks and, in the misty distance, the massive coastal formation of Double Point.

Plan to arrive at low tide. Clamber down the trail to the creek, then crawl on your hands and knees through Sea Tunnel, a rough-cut arch through which Coast Creek plunges to the ocean, and then wander the beach below the overlook. The cliffs, excellent examples of the sharply folded sedimentary rocks common at Point Reyes, are gilded with gold and ocher lichen, and in spring and summer are washed with pink and yellow blooms of tiny succulents.

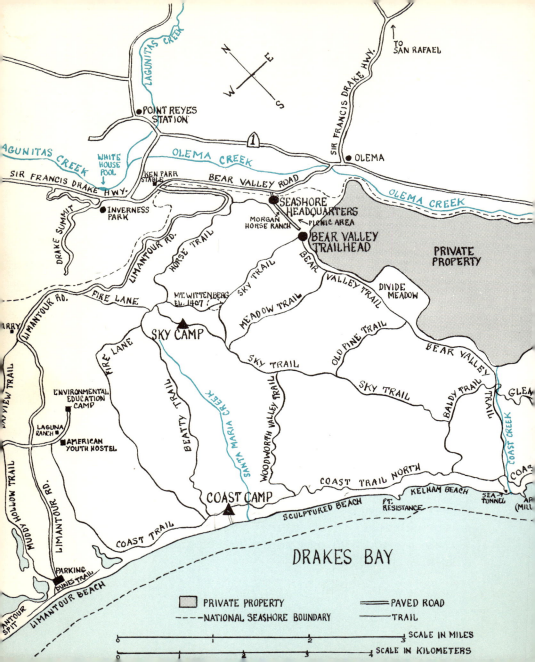

TRAIL DISTANCES

Bear Valley Trailhead to:

	Miles	Km.
Arch Rock	4.4	7.0
Coast Camp	8.0	12.8
Divide Meadow	1.5	2.4
Double Point	9.0	14.4
Glen Camp	4.6	7.4
Palomarin Trailhead	11.9	19.0
Sky Camp	2.5	4.0
Wildcat Camp	6.7	10.7

Palomarin Trailhead to:

	Miles	Km.
Arch Rock	8.1	13.0
Bass Lake	2.5	4.0
Bear Valley Trailhead	11.9	19.0
Coast Camp	12.5	20.0
Double Point	4.0	6.4
Glen Camp	7.2	11.5
Pablo Point	3.9	6.2
Wildcat Camp	5.2	8.3

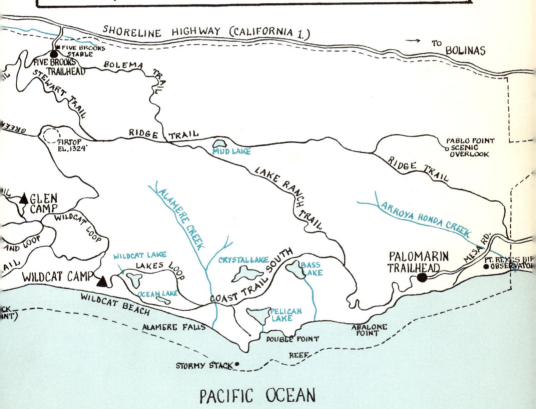

Across Coast Creek to the south is a narrow beach with rocky, wave-washed outcroppings crusted with blue mussels. Here are tide pools teeming with snails, limpets, starfish and anemones. Look at and photograph, but do not disturb, these tidal colonies. Step carefully on the wet rocks; the amber-colored kelp that coats them is glassy slick.

Kelham Beach. If you reach Arch Rock at high tide, walk a mile north on Coast Trail to an easy path down the cliffs to this pleasant beach, a safe sunning spot where cormorants cluster on off-shore stacks and sandpipers skitter at the surf's edge.

Sky Trail. As you hike Bear Valley Trail to the coast, you pass several trail intersections. First is Sky Trail, a much-used, steep, two-mile climb through the forest of Inverness Ridge to the brushy slopes of Mount Wittenberg. A half-mile drop west of the ridge brings you to Sky Camp, located in a broad meadow, where certain camp sites are sheltered by tall firs. Here you may spot a flight of bluebirds, flashing sapphire in the sun; watch a flock of band-tailed pigeons wheel in the timbered canyon below; search the meadow for wildflowers which bloom much of the year on this often foggy mountainside; climb Mount Wittenberg; or stroll up the hill north of the camp, for views of the ocean and esteros.

Sky Trail also rides the crest of Inverness Ridge south from Limantour Road. From Sky Camp, you can walk a mile or more north, through groves of bays, firs and pines, through meadows thick with lupine and thistles, to the trailhead at the summit of Limantour Road. Sky Trail also winds south for four miles through the center of the fir forest, eventually emerges on the brushy hills that surround Baldy Mountain and then swings down to Coast Trail near Kelham Beach.

Fire Lane Trail. Departing from Sky Trail .8 of a mile south of Limantour Road summit, Fire Lane winds four miles down to the coast through meadows, clumps of fir and Bishop pine, up and over rounded timbered knolls, and finally into marshy coastal meadows where ducks swoop in winter.

Beatty Trail. This old ranch road traverses three miles of up-and-down terrain between Sky Trail and Coast Camp and crosses wide meadows, brushy regions where you are almost sure to see deer and coveys of California quail. Beatty winds through fir groves — look in tree crotches to

Divide Meadows.

see the masses of moss, lichen and twigs that are nests for packrats — then across vast, open areas dotted with gray-green rock formations. Across the hills are vistas of Drake's Bay and the sea.

Woodworth Valley Trail. Departing from Sky Trail in the midst of a deep forest, Woodworth Valley Trail travels downhill through a beautiful tree-rimmed grassy swale. Beyond this clearing the path is in lightly wooded country and then edges a deep, forested canyon. Near a huge rock spotted with orange and green lichen you emerge suddenly to a spectacular view of Limantour, Drake's Bay and, gleaming in the western distance, Point Reyes Beach and the Pacific. As the trail plunges downhill, the view expands to include Double Point, far to the south. The intersection with Coast Trail is 1.7 miles from Sky Trail; a path down to the surf-dashed rocks of Sculptured Beach is only a few yards ahead.

Meadow Trail. This path climbs 2.3 miles up the ridge from Bear Valley Trail to intersect with Sky Trail near Sky Camp. Special features are giant, multi-trunked bay trees; a half-mile-long oval meadow ringed with firs and carpeted with flowers and ferns; and, near the intersection with Sky Trail, distant views across a forested canyon.

Old Pine Trail. So-named because of an isolated grove of Bishop pine in the dense fir forest, Old Pine leaves Bear Valley Trail at Divide Meadow to ascend the ridge for two miles to junction with Sky Trail. The narrow, exceptionally

Old Pine Trail.

wooded path threads through ancient Douglas firs that sprout lush fern gardens in mossy bends of trunks and branches. The upper reaches of Old Pine are lined with huckleberry bushes higher than your head, and the crop is at its prime in September.

Baldy Trail. This lightly traveled trail leaves Bear Valley Trail at the intersection with Glen Trail and Coast Creek, climbs steeply through forest and ferns for a half mile, then opens into a spreading, irregular meadow, dotted with tall firs and sheltered by the rounded slopes of Baldy from the winds of the nearby coast. This meadow is a good picnic spot when Arch Rock is in fog. Between the meadow and Sky Trail intersection, Baldy Trail is open and hedged with coyote bush, a favorite browsing place for deer.

61

Coast Trail, North

Coast Trail follows the shore from Limantour Beach on the north to the Park's southern border at Palomarin and offers hikers close looks at some of Point Reyes' most remarkable, most remote coastal scenery. Though occasionally rough and rocky, Coast Trail is popular with bicyclists.

Short hikes on the northern section of Coast Trail include: a stroll from Limantour parking area as far south on the beach as whim entices you — perhaps past a marshy meadow with thousands of birds, then up through the dunes to intersect with Coast Trail. Or, for less beach walking and a more intimate glance at the marsh, amble from Laguna Ranch Hostel down to the beach and Coast Trail. Coast Camp, tucked behind tall ocean-side cliffs, sits beside Coast Trail at the southern tip of Limantour Beach.

Sculptured Beach. A half-mile south of Coast Camp is Sculptured Beach, a fascinating rocky, reefy stretch complete with caves, tunnels and a distinctive stack, Devil's Thumb. Accessible from the beach at low tide and from Coast Trail at high tide, Sculptured Beach is three to four miles (depending on your route) from Limantour and Laguna and is popular with artists, photographers and tide-pool prowlers.

South of the beach Coast Trail traverses open headlands above Kelham Beach, swings past Arch Rock and intersects with Bear Valley Trail. Four major trails intersect with this northern section of Coast Trail: Fire Lane, Beatty, Woodworth Valley and Sky Trails.

SOUTHERN TRAILS:
FIVE BROOKS AND PALOMARIN TRAILHEADS

Coast Trail, South
As Coast Trail climbs the cliffs south of Arch Rock, it plunges into wilder, more remote coastal country than that north of the popular Bear Valley Trail, and terminates at Palomarin Trailhead.

Glen Trail. The first major intersection on the southern portion of Coast Trail is with Glen Trail. This wooded path is the main access route from Bear Valley to Glen Camp, which is set inland from the ocean's persistent moisture in a quiet, peaceful valley.

Highland Loop, Wildcat Loop. These trails are partly forested, partly brushy paths that offer hikers alternate routes or opportunities for circle trips through the country that lies between Glen Camp and the ocean. You have tantalizing glimpses of the surf as Coast Trail drops down a long, forested canyon toward the ocean and the open coastal area near Wildcat Camp.

Alamere Falls. Hike south along Wildcat Beach to see Point Reyes' only significant waterfall. In spring and early summer, when Alamere Creek runs full, the falls sheet over high cliffs to the beach below.

Wildcat Lake. As Coast Trail climbs away from Wildcat Beach, it passes Wildcat Lake, a sixty-foot-deep fresh-water lake that is popular with ducks but too dangerous for people. Because of steep drop-offs and exceptionally cold water, no swimming is permitted here or in any of the other fresh-water lakes in this region of the Seashore. These lakes, formed by natural dams caused by the earth's faulting and slipping, are picturesque but hazardous.

South of Wildcat Lake, you can choose between the high cliff route of Coast Trail, which has sweeping ocean views and a cut-off to the beach near Alamere Falls or, in case of fog, the shorter inland Coast Trail, a one-time ranch road.

Lakes Loop. This trail circles through the headlands, passes a few small lakes and includes the cliff and inland routes of Coast Trail.

Double Point. Whichever route you choose, swing toward the ocean at Pelican Lake and hike up the headlands to overlook Double Point. You stand five hundred feet above the surf, on the lip of a curved cove that is edged with a crescent beach and pointed at each tip with tumbled, rocky stacks. While the rocks are alive with birds, Double Point's prime natural wonders are its harbor seals. This is a major rookery and the seals, gleaming wet in the sun, lie in windrows along the beach and rocky reefs below.

The view from Double Point is one of the most exciting in the Seashore. North are the Bear Valley Coast, Limantour, Drake's Bay and the white cliffs. South are Duxbury Reef and Bolinas. West is Point Reyes Promontory, Chimney Rock and the entrance to Drake's Bay. To the southwest lie the open ocean, and, out to sea, the Farallon Islands.

Pelican Lake.

This also is a prime place to see the effect of the earth's folding and faulting. Notice the almost vertical slices of soil, some clay-colored against white rock, in the coastal hills to the north and east.

Pelican Lake. No pelicans, but flocks of sea gulls circle above this chilly tarn which lies behind the high cliffs of Double Point. Fed by underground springs and dammed by the earth's sagging, the lake is only a few hundred feet above the sea — the closest fresh-water lake to the ocean in all of California.

From Double Point, Coast Trail continues south past tree-rimmed Bass Lake, a good site for a picnic or rest, passes the old Lake Ranch residence and winds down a steep road through brush headlands to the Palomarin Trailhead.

Lake Ranch Trail

Two miles north of Palomarin Trailhead, Lake Ranch Trail leaves Coast Trail, then angles north through meadows fringed with fir. It provides fine views of Double Point, the coastal lakes and, as it climbs higher, of Drake's Bay and the ocean. The forest becomes thicker and fernier; lichen and moss drape giant Douglas firs.

Mud Lake. An ideal location to observe the busy life of a forest pond is at Mud Lake, three miles above the ranch on Lake Ranch Trail. Frogs squeak and plop in water green with massed pond weeds; wood ducks paddle about in still pools; and dragon flies shimmer in the sun above the cattails. A half mile north of Mud Lake, Lake Ranch Trail ends in a magnificent grove of old firs on Ridge Trail.

Ridge Trail

This long trail, which spans the crest of Inverness Ridge in the Seashore's southern region, departs on the east side of Mesa Road opposite the Point Reyes Bird Observatory. The path climbs through coyote bush, manzanita and sage, then through young forest for 3.3 miles to an intersection with the trail to Pablo Point.

Pablo Point. The Point trail doubles south and winds 1.7 miles through forest to the high, open meadow of Pablo Point Overlook. Views here are of Mount Tamalpais and Bolinas Lagoon.

From Pablo Point, Ridge Trail continues north for 4.2 miles through old and new fir forest — an exceptionally fine region in which to observe both forest and grassland birds — to the beautiful grove and trail intersection which marks the end of Lake Ranch Trail.

Bolema Trail

Popular with horse parties, Bolema Trail is a steep route that leads uphill from Five Brooks Trailhead through the wooded eastern slope of Inverness Ridge to intersect Ridge Trail.

Stewart Trail

Stewart Trail, a one-time logging road, twists west and then south from Five Brooks Trailhead to Ridge Trail passing through the Douglas fir forest cut over in the 1950's. Because of the mild, year-round growing season, the logging scars are fast disappearing, and Stewart Trail is a broad, green road through a few towering old firs, soft downy young ones, old clumps of California Bay and the typical forest undergrowth of huckleberries, ferns and wildflowers.

Greenpicker Trail

Ridge Trail continues north along the crest to circle Firtop, a 1324-foot wooded knoll. Here, in a summit meadow a mile and a quarter beyond the intersection with Stewart Trail, is Greenpicker Trail, a narrow, ferny, grown-in path favored by horsemen as an alternate route from Five Brooks. Beyond this intersection, Ridge Trail doubles south for a mile and a half, to intersect with Coast Trail one mile south of Glen Camp.

Back Country Camps

Sky Camp. Perched high on the slopes of Mount Wittenberg, surrounded by flower-strewn meadows and punctuated by a grove of tall firs, Sky Camp has remarkable views but frequently is windswept and foggy.

Glen Camp. Tucked in a small inland valley dotted with century-old live oaks and giant firs, Glen Camp often is warm and sunny when coastal areas are wrapped in fog. Bring insect repellent; flies sometimes swarm here on rare warm days. Also, hang your pack high, beyond the reach of raiding raccoons.

Coast Camp. Set behind tall coastal cliffs above Santa Maria Beach, Coast Camp is near the rocks and tide pools of Sculptured Beach.

Wildcat Camp. Reserved for groups, this camp sits on a broad shelf above a wide, white beach. Nearby is Wildcat Creek, its banks shimmering with bright green watercress, its mouth clogged with bleached driftwood. From the beach, which has a gentle slope and usually is safe for wading, you have views north to Arch Rock and south to Double Point.

Camp Facilities

Sky, Glen and Coast camps each have twelve sites. Each site accommodates as many as eight people and includes a picnic table with benches, a charcoal brazier and grill, and space for tents. These camps have drinking water, restrooms and a hitch-rail for horses.

Wildcat Camp has six sites, each accommodating twenty people. Each site has two long tables plus two charcoal braziers and grills. Restrooms, water and a hitch-rail are provided.

Camping Regulations

Camp rules include: no dogs or other pets, and no fireworks or firearms, including air rifles. Fires are restricted to charcoal braziers or gas stoves. Wood fires may be built on beaches, away from grassy or swimming areas, when driftwood is available. Campsites must be cleaned before campers depart.

No fees are charged for the sites, but they are in great demand, especially on weekends, and stays are limited to one night. Reservations may be made one month ahead at Bear Valley Information Center. Campers are required to register at Bear Valley, and to pick up camping permits showing that they have reserved campsites before setting off on hikes.

Though the back country camps are remote, National Park Service personnel visit them daily and are available to answer questions or offer assistance. For more information about the camps, write or phone the Bear Valley Information Center.

5.   OUTSIDE THE SEASHORE

Olema

The closest village to Bear Valley Headquarters, Olema was in past years a sportsmen's center boasting a hotel and as many as nine saloons. Today this crossroads community has a few small restaurants and shops.

North on California 1, past the turn for Bear Valley, is the privately owned Olema Ranch Campground. The only auto camp near the Seashore with trailer hookups, it is a site favored by recreational vehicle owners. Bicycles are also for rent here.

Point Reyes Station

Now a ranching community on California 1 a half dozen miles north of Olema, Point Reyes Station originally was a station for the narrow gauge railroad that shuttled dairy products and lumber between San Francisco and Tomales. In addition to small restaurants and variety stores, Point Reyes Station has a bank, a service station and a garage.

Inverness

Inverness, on Sir Francis Drake Highway six miles north of Bear Valley Headquarters, began life in 1889 as a resort village. Small tracts of land were sold for summer cottages, but the project was not a success and Inverness, said to have been named by a homesick Scottish rancher, languished until the 1906 quake. Then San Francisco families rushed to buy lots and build summer homes — insurance against being homeless after another temblor. Ironically, the San Andreas Fault was at their doorsteps — in Tomales Bay, a few yards from Inverness' main street. Today, Inverness is a quiet village with a few motels, restaurants, a grocery store and a service station.

Tomales Bay State Park

Set on the protected western shore of Tomales Bay, three miles north of Inverness off Tomales Point Road, Tomales Bay State Park is most often visited for its small, pleasant swimming beaches. On summer days, water in Tomales Bay sometimes reaches 70 degrees, and ocean fog frequently is held back by Inverness Ridge.

Heart's Desire Beach is a short walk from the parking area, and wooded trails lead to Pebble, Indian and Shell beaches. Park facilities include restrooms, a picnic area with tables and charcoal braziers. No dogs are permitted on the beaches and must be leashed in other areas. A fee of $1 per car is charged, and rangers are on duty daily.

Bolinas

Bolinas Lagoon, near the Seashore's southern border, was in Mexican times a harbor for British, American and Russian ships searching for sea otters. In later years, the village that sprang up along this cove became a timber port and eventually a seaside resort. Today Bolinas has a motel and several restaurants and variety stores.

Point Reyes Bird Observatory

This private, non-profit corporation of amateur and profes-
sional ornithologists has headquarters within the Seashore
off Mesa Road a half mile south of Palomarin Trailhead.
Members engage in research projects and cooperate with
the National Park Service in year-round study of bird life at
the Seashore.

Audubon Canyon Ranch

Each spring, great blue herons and plumed egrets come to
nest in the tall redwoods of Audubon Canyon Ranch, located on Bolinas Lagoon, a few miles south of the Seashore
border on California 1.

For an exceptionally fine view of the birds and their
young, hike a half mile up to Henderson Overlook, a quiet
spot complete with benches and built-in binoculars. From
this vantage point, you can look down upon the birds
nesting in the tops of trees which grow in the gorge below.

A joint project of the Marin, Golden Gate and Sequoia
Audubon Societies, the ranch is open to the public from
March 1 through July 4, Saturdays, Sundays and holidays,
10 A.M. to 4 P.M. Groups are asked to visit Tuesday through
Friday and to phone for appointments. No admission is
charged and facilities include a bookshop and a picnic area.

6. ADDITIONAL INFORMATION AND REGULATIONS

Accommodations and Services

No motels, stores or gas stations are located within the Seashore. The only restaurant is the Seashore Snack Bar at Drake's Beach, open 11 A.M. to 5 P.M. daily, weather permitting, throughout the year except Thanksgiving, Christmas and New Year's Day.

Camping

The only camping in the Seashore is at primitive back country camps which are reached by trail. Campsites are free but are limited and in demand. Reservations may be made one month in advance. Write or phone Bear Valley Information Center for reservations and information.

Samuel P. Taylor State Park in Lagunitas, six miles from Bear Valley Headquarters, has camping facilities. Reservations are necessary and may be made through Ticketron or by writing the Reservations Office, California Department of Parks and Recreation, P.O. Box 2390, Sacramento, Calif. 95811.

Olema Ranch Campground, a half mile north of Olema, is the only area campground offering trailer hookups.

Dogs

Dogs (except seeing-eye dogs) and other pets are not permitted on Seashore trails. Leashed dogs may visit Point Reyes Beach and the non-swimming areas of Limantour and Drake's beaches.

Emergencies

For emergencies of all types, see the telephone numbers at the end of this book.

Fees

No fees are charged for admission, participation in naturalist programs or use of campgrounds within the Seashore.

Fires

Charcoal braziers with grills are provided at back country camps; no wood fires are permitted in these areas. Grates and rings for charcoal fires are available at Point Reyes Beach. Beach fires (driftwood is scarce) are permitted away from swimming and grassy areas.

Fishing

A California fishing license is required of every angler over 15 years old. Licenses and booklets explaining details of California regulations — for fresh, salt-water and shellfish — are available at grocery and variety stores. Also, ask at Bear Valley Information Center for a free "Fishing Information" sheet prepared by National Park Service personnel.

Hazards

Point Reyes has no poisonous snakes, no dangerous animals and mosquitoes rarely are a problem. The most annoying plants are nettles and poison oak. In autumn, the oak glows red and often bears transparent berries. Beware! Do not pick!

Seashore cliffs are steep and usually are composed of a loose, crumbly rock. Stay back from cliff edges and do not attempt to climb up or down from beaches. Use marked trails.

Since many beaches are under water at high tide, keep track of the time you spend beachcombing. Know the tide table — ask at Headquarters or consult local newspapers.

Hunting

No hunting is permitted within the Seashore. All guns, even air rifles, are prohibited.

Surfing

Surfers, usually clad in wet suits because of the cold water, sometimes ride the gentle swells off Limantour and Drake's beaches. All other beaches have violent surf, undertow or concealed rocks.

Swimming

Only Drake's and Limantour beaches are reasonably safe for swimming and wading. Drake's Beach has a bathhouse, but neither beach has lifeguards. Never, even in calm areas, leave children unattended.

Other Sports

Bicycles are for rent at Olema Ranch Campground. Though Bear Valley and Coast trails have rough and rutted spots, they are the only Seashore trails suitable for biking. No motor bikes are permitted on trails.

Riding horses and ricks for hay-rides are for rent at Five Brooks Stables, three miles south of Olema on California 1. Ken Parr Stables, a mile north of Bear Valley Headquarters on Bear Valley Road, rents riding horses. Before planning a horse trip, check at Bear Valley Information Center. Certain Seashore trails are reserved for foot traffic.

Memorial to Sir Francis Drake near the mouth of Drake's Estero.

7. TELEPHONE NUMBERS AND ADDRESSES

POINT REYES NATIONAL SEASHORE

The buildings below are open every day, year-round, during hours shown:

Bear Valley Information Center
Point Reyes, Calif. 94956

Phone: (415) 663-1092
Hours: 8 A.M. to 5 P.M.

Kenneth C. Patrick Information
Center (Drake's Beach)
Point Reyes, Calif. 94956

Phone: (415) 669-1250
Hours: 8 A.M. to 5 P.M.
      (summer)
Winter hours variable

Laguna Ranch American Youth
Hostel
P.O. Box 59
Point Reyes, Calif. 94956

Phone: (415) 669-9985
Hours: 4:30 P.M. to 9 A.M.

EMERGENCY NUMBERS:

The following phones are answered at all times throughout the year:

National Park Service Ranger
Bear Valley Information Center

Phone: (415) 663-1092

California Highway Patrol

Phone: (415) 831-2000

Marin County Sheriff

Phone: (415) 479-2311 or
       ENterprise 1-1560